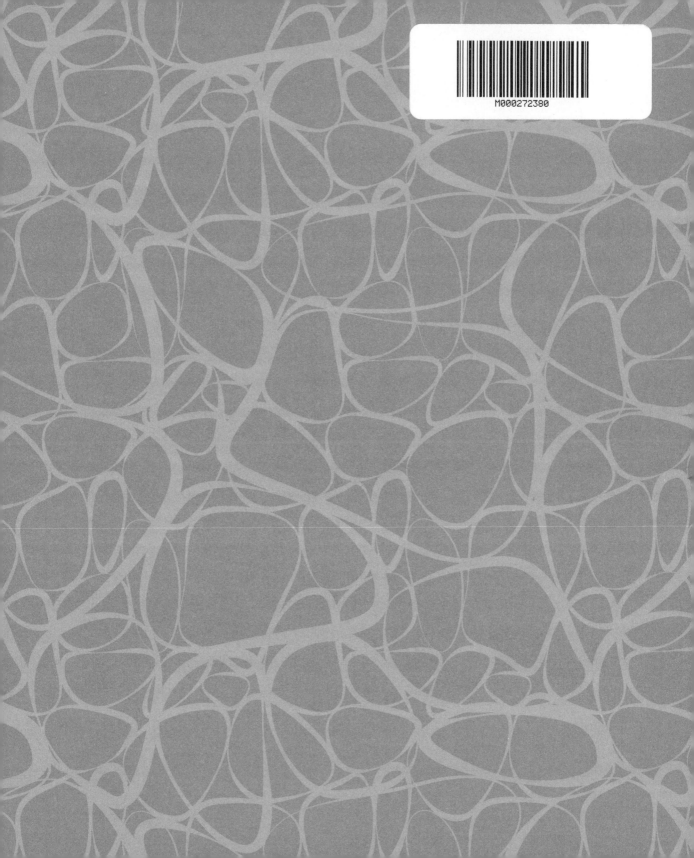

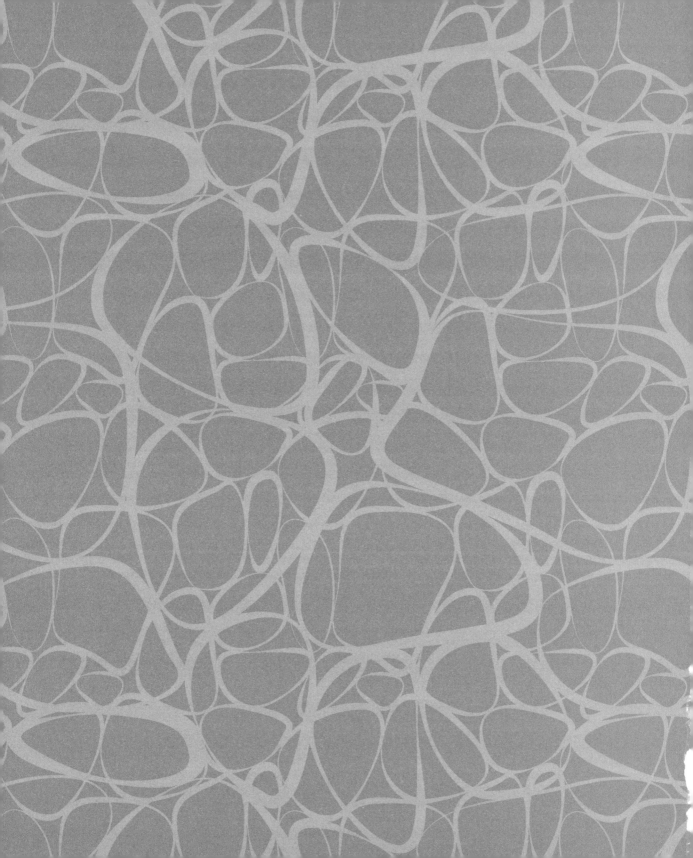

How the FRENCH Live

How the FRENCH Live

MODERN FRENCH STYLE

SIHAM MAZOUZ

CURATOR OF **FRENCH BY DESIGN**

GIBBS SMITH
TO ENRICH AND INSPIRE HUMANKIND

Contents

INTRODUCTION

Our family moved nine years ago from Provence, southern France, to the United States, first to Charlotte, North Carolina, and then to San Francisco, California. We haven't dramatically changed our way of living since we moved away from our homeland. We have kept our family habits, instill the same values to our kids, and eaten the same diet. Even in the way we decorated our first American home, we followed the same principle we always had: less house, more home. Less lawn manicuring, and more time spent outdoors to build family memories on sunny days. Less new furniture buying, more thrifting and repurposing the old and making it new again.

It seems to me that American friends I have made tended to envision French decorating style as "chateau-esque" or shabby chic rustic. While this used to be true, the rule has changed. Modern French families tend to mix and match décor elements from different eras and styles to create unique interiors that represents them. They don't furnish their homes to follow a trend or to impress visitors. They want their homes to represent their lifestyle; they add elements of their travels or inherited pieces that remind them of their family experience and speak to them.

The French have a particular affection for the old and antiques, and they despise total-look interiors. You will rarely see matching sets in a living room, but rather an antique sofa with a Scandinavian modern armchair or an ethnic rug. *Au revoir* to grandma's armoires and matching buffets: if these are used in modern interiors, they are usually painted a bold, unexpected color to create a modern look and fit the space. Neither do we French like symmetry in our interiors. You'll rarely see a sofa flanked by matching chairs or end tables with identical table lamps.

All of these differences between French style and what I often see in American homes have made me wonder whether we, the French, have a common way of decorating and living as families regardless of whether we live in the motherland or are exiled from the French hexagon and live as expatriates. To answer my own question and to photograph and write this book, I visited fourteen French families living in France or abroad. This threw me outside of my comfort zone on many levels: reaching out via email to perfect strangers found via Instagram, personal blogs or contacted through referrals; knocking on their doors across the world from where I live; and shooting their interiors and interviewing them. And something pretty amazing happened! Not only have I realized that there is indeed a French way of living but I also witnessed the French culture in action. Most of the lovely families that agreed to participate in this book not only opened up their homes and private world to me but also showed me what the French culture is all about: for example, families with young children or even teenagers rarely miss a dinner meal together. Rarely did I leave these homes without an invitation to stay over and share a simple meal and a glass of wine after the photo shoot was over. That's the French way for you: a meal is not just a meal, it's a way to show a connection, to share a special bonding moment. I will be forever grateful to these families for reminding me how genuine and gracious my native culture is.

None of the interiors was styled by a professional interior designer. I wanted this book to be authentic, to show real interiors and real families. In a world of perfectly styled pictures, I felt I needed to be true to these families and their own style so that you, the reader, can get a true view of how the French live. I hope these house tours will help you decorate your home without feeling tied to rules of interior design. In all the chapters presented, a common philosophy the owners was "My home looks like me." Let's say no to total-look interiors that might look pretty on paper but lack soul and personality, and yes to interiors that feel natural and authentic, that gather décor elements with meaning, be they inherited family pieces of furniture or objects

that remind one of a family travel escape. Less house, more home—the French way.

Of course, I couldn't have written a book about French families without mentioning the importance of food in the French culture. In France, meals are not just a way to feed oneself; they are a staple of the culture: a meal can last for hours—people share and argue over sensitive topics. Meals are a way to connect, to exchange, to build memories. I therefore asked each family to share their signature recipe, a simple recipe they like to make for special occasions, or comfort food they like to cook for their loved ones. At the end of each chapter, the family shares an easy recipe with you. Go ahead, cook, and tell your family that tonight you're having a meal together, without cell phones or tablets at the table. Reconnect with your loved ones; because, in the end, those simple moments are what home and family truly means.

Lastly, I want to thank all the sweet families who opened up their homes—and souls—to participate in this amazing project (with a special nod to their pets, who played unexpected models and literally posed for my camera); my family for their support—my husband for rearranging his business travel schedule to take care of our beloved golden retriever, Miss Daisy, and our daughters—and my two teenage girls for staying out of trouble and being trustworthy while I was traveling abroad. I also want to thank Madge, my dear editor, for keeping me on schedule while gently holding my hand throughout the project, and the Gibbs Smith team for giving me full creative freedom in the execution of this project. I will be forever grateful for their trust and support.

Vanessa + Ceki

SAINT-RÉMY-DE-PROVENCE, FRANCE

VANESSA, CEKI, MARCELO, AMALYA AND LIOR live in London, but it's their family summer retreat home we're visiting in this chapter. It was a lifelong dream for Vanessa to have a family home where the extended family (Ceki's family lives in Turkey) could gather and create memories.

Nested in a little hamlet five minutes away from Saint-Rémy-de-Provence and Les Baux-de-Provence, the family home is located on a two-and-a-half-acre property and is generously open to the outdoors. Vanessa and Ceki remodeled the house entirely—and added an extension—with a main idea in mind: live freely indoors and out, and enjoy quality time together.

Vanessa and Ceki are globetrotters; they jump on every chance to travel around the world, and feel that having kids should not stop one from exploring the world. They actually feel the opposite. From their earliest childhood, Marcelo, eleven, Amalya, eight, and little Lior, four, have been exposed to the world through travel adventures. When the family moved from New York to London in 2007, they took a six-month sabbatical to travel the world.

Vanessa shares her tips and travel adventures with children on her blog, BozAround. She also loves to bring back treasures and décor pieces from the family trips, and jokingly confesses that a few times Ceki had to reluctantly carry fragile pieces on top of his head during plane rides so they wouldn't get stepped on.

Vanessa and Ceki's home is filled with their travel finds and family inherited pieces. From one room to another, African art plays with Indian textiles, Moroccan rugs and antiques scouted locally. There is no rule in Vanessa's approach to decorating; when she's showing you her summer home her eyes glitter, because every piece has a special place in her heart: from travel purchases to her grandmother's bedside table and her mom's painting in the media room, everything is there to remind her of amazing memories and people that matter to her.

When they renovated the house, Vanessa even made a trip to Istanbul to bring back antique copper and marble sinks, which she had fitted for the bathrooms throughout the house. She felt it was important to rescue pieces from Ceki's cultural heritage. The vegetal-fiber hammock in the master bedroom patio room was a piece Vanessa bought in Venezuela while doing an internship there, and she confesses that it took twenty years for this hammock to find its home: this is the piece she sees every morning from her bed when she wakes up, and it makes her happy.

The kids have a blast when they come to their summer home, exploring acres of the outdoors and playing by the water stream that runs through the property. There are also a trampoline, a tippy, a pool, a soccer field, and a pond for catch-and-release fishing.

When they are not exploring the beautiful region and villages nearby, the family tries to spend as much time together near home as they possibly can: they ride their bikes to the village, cook planchas and barbecues, and play board games in the evenings. And then friends and family come to visit, from Vanessa's mom, from Paris, to Ceki's brother and sister, from Turkey. Vanessa loves the idea that this home is where memories are being built. In total, the house offers twelve beds to accommodate visitors.

Their favorite rooms in the house are the kitchen—open to a gorgeous shaded patio—and the family room, with its unique and vibrant yellow color accents. All meals are shared together, but one meal is more important than others—the breakfast. Ceki cherishes the Turkish tradition of having a big, dishes-filled table for breakfast, and the family enjoys hours of breakfast time in the morning. Vanessa also enjoys preparing simple foods; she gets a regular vegetable and fruit delivery from a farmer so she can cook her meals with the best local ingredients.

Vanessa and Ceki's summer home celebrates the simple pleasures of slow life and easy living: good food, family time, outdoor activities and areas all over the property to lounge and relax, with the soft sound of the singing cicadas.

Vanessa designed this gorgeous kitchen herself, sourcing green vintage-style tiles from Morocco and pumpkin-shaped light fixtures in a local Provence shop. The kitchen is open to the patio for an easy flow between indoors and outdoors.

Vanessa and Ceki's living room is the favorite family place
for playing board games and hanging out. The piano, which
Marcelo, Vanessa's first-born son, plays wonderfully, is one
of Vanessa's cherished family inheritance pieces. The organic
rattan décor elements add a typical southern French mood to
the living space.

ABOVE: Small accessories in the entryway add an organic character to the house.

RIGHT: The home office, also imagined by Vanessa, features a locally scouted vintage desk, French rustic wooden chairs and a graphic-tiled floor that mimics a rug.

Two guest rooms are always ready to host extra beds, since this vacation home is all about connecting with family and loved ones. In one guest room, above, Vanessa used a vintage table to hold a Turkish copper vessel, transforming the pair into a unique sink. The global panache of these rooms is consistent with the décor in the rest of the house.

Vanessa and Ceki's master bedroom features an open plan with an earthy, organic bathroom area. The ensemble feels like a luxurious yet laid-back vacation spot.

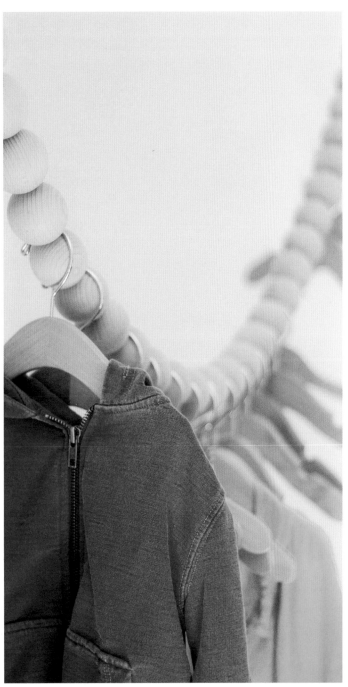

In the South of France, locals spend a lot of time outside enjoying the perfect weather. Vanessa and Ceki wanted their home to be opened to the outdoors and spend a lot of time hanging out in their beautiful shaded patio.

GREEN BEANS WITH GARLIC AND TOMATOES

Here is a simple green bean recipe Vanessa loves to cook for her family. She likes to serve this dish with a roasted chicken.

SERVES 5

4 garlic cloves, minced

2 tablespoons olive oil

3 fresh organic tomatoes

2 $\frac{1}{2}$ pounds fresh green beans (the larger, the better)

Salt and pepper

In a saucepan over medium heat, cook the minced garlic in the olive oil, making sure the garlic doesn't brown.

Cut the tomatoes in large quarters and add them to the pan.

Cut off the green bean ends with scissors and rinse the beans. (Do not cut the beans lengthwise.)

Add the green beans to the pan.

Cover the pan and reduce the heat to low. Let the vegetables cook for 1 to 1 $\frac{1}{2}$ hours on reduced heat. Check the cooking progress often and gently turn the beans and tomatoes. Be careful not to crush the tomatoes too much, as you want to avoid making a sauce at the bottom of the pan.

Season with salt and pepper to taste.

Ilaria + Jérôme

AIX-EN-PROVENCE, FRANCE

ILARIA, HER HUSBAND, JÉRÔME, and their two sons, Thomas and Tristan, left Paris three years ago to move to the South of France. Ilaria was originally from Milan, and after thirteen years in Paris, she and Jérôme were thrilled at the prospect of life in sunny Provence; but finding a home in the coveted city of Aix-en-Provence was no joke. Eighteen months of intense searching led them to this 1970s home located near the Parc Jourdan.

At first, the 1,290-square-foot property seemed outdated and charmless, having never been remodeled since its 1969 construction. But Ilaria saw a huge potential: the natural light and the patio and garden the house featured. The family embarked on a two-month remodeling, during which Ilaria connected with local craftsmen to renovate the space: walls were taken down to allow a free flow of natural light, electricity and plumbing were updated to code, and the original parquet was sanded three times to give it a modern look. Ilaria worked extensively on letting the natural light in and opened up the space to allow a more natural flow between the indoors and outdoors.

In the living areas, which receive lots of light, she chose to canvas the walls in white and then progressively added touches of color. In the darker areas, like the hallway and the private rooms, she chose a darker color palette: a deep petroleum-blue paint punctuates the space as a *parti pris* for the lack of natural light.

In her decorating, Ilaria worked with the furniture and accessories she already had. She didn't want to acquire a lot of new things. "I wanted the house to feel like a vacation home, where pieces can be moved within the interior throughout the seasons, and also moved indoors and outdoors," confides Ilaria. So she carefully added elements that would remind her of a vacation home: the woven pendant light over the dining space, storage baskets, and plants add a Mediterranean feel to her Scandinavian furniture and accessories.

The kitchen got a major design lift. Ilaria worked with local craftsmen to create a modern kitchen, open to the living space, without the constraints of smelly odors diffusing into the living area. Jérôme, a native of Lyon—a region known for its love of good food—enjoys cooking, so the couple opted for a sliding glass and wooden door that allows a visual flow but inhibits the smells and fumes of cooking food. The kitchen cabinet structures are generic, from a major Swedish retailer, but Ilaria had the façades custom made in an exotic wood called frake from West Africa; she loved the texture so much that she decided to keep them unfinished. Her countertops are Corian, an easy material to clean and maintain. The divider between the living room and the entryway is also made from frake wood, keeping consistency.

The family spends all dinners together as a way of catching up with everyone's lives. Weekends are also cherished as family time, whether it's embarking on a road trip to the beach or walking around the beautiful city of Aix-en-Provence. While Jérôme works long hours on weekdays in Marseille, a neighboring city, Ilaria works from home as an interior design consultant. This enables her to customize her schedule around her kids' lives: picking up her younger son Tristan from school or catching up with both boys during snack time after school.

I spent a fun-filled morning with Ilaria in her home, and her contagious energy was palpable. Her home is just like she is: carefree, grounded, and filled with positive energy.

Ilaria masterfully mixes Scandinavian pieces with a Mediterranean flair. She recently updated the upholstery of a vintage chair to embrace the urban jungle trend and give the interior an "exterior" feel. The French spend a lot of time outdoors, and a garden is usually seen as an extra outdoor room of the house. The TV, an eyesore according to Ilaria, can easily be hidden behind the rolling plant when not in use.

To separate the living space from the private rooms, Ilaria worked with local craftsmen to build an open flow and create shelving for the family's book collection. The hallway leading to the sleeping area desperately lacks natural light, so Ilaria made the decision of going darker, choosing a very dark midnight blue paint to create a cozy mood. The gorgeous chevron wooden floors throughout the house add a French foundation to this eclectic space.

Ilaria + Jérôme 41

Ilaria and Jérôme dedicated an entire wall of their master bedroom to the family's musical instruments. Ilaria chose a royal blue color and some simple, discreet shelves for storing instruments and scores.

Thomas's room showcases a soft green palette and clean-lined furniture. Shelves running along an entire wall ensure a clutter-free floor. Because of the orientation of the room, Ilaria chose an accent color and keep the rest white to take optimum advantage of the natural light.

Tristan's room is more of a play laboratory, with an extensive collection of miniature toys, books and games. Ilaria chose a paler blue color splash, carefully placed, to accent the walls. She again kept some walls white to reflect natural light.

Ilaria and Jérôme's bedroom displays a neutral palette, inviting relaxation. On the opposite wall, the dark blue niche dedicated to musical instruments contrasts dramatically with this white side of the room. Linen is Ilaria's favorite texture for bedding, and here the bed is simply dressed to induce sleep. Ilaria loves to move her potted plants inside and out, depending on the season.

The patio, with original terrazzo flooring, serves as a liaison between the living room and the garden. Furniture, plants and decorative pieces can be moved in and out according to Ilaria's mood.

SHRIMP, AVOCADO AND GRAPEFRUIT SUMMER SALAD

Made with simple ingredients and without using any oven or heat, this healthy and fresh summer salad is simple and very tasty.

SERVES 4

2 cups cooked medium-sized shrimp

Juice of 1 lime

2 avocados

2 grapefruits

½ cup minced coriander*

Soy sauce

  * Cilantro.

Peel the shrimp and set aside in a bowl. Squeeze the juice of a lime over the shrimp and toss.

Cut the avocados into small squares.

Peel and cut the grapefruits.

Combine all ingredients in a bowl and top with the minced cilantro and soy sauce to taste. Reserve in the fridge for up to an hour before serving.

Chloé + Mehdi

MAR VISTA, LOS ANGELES, CALIFORNIA

CHLOÉ FLEURY IS A RENOWNED prop stylist and French illustrator. Her portfolio includes clients such as McDonald's, Gap, Target and Warner Brothers. When she was a teenager living in Lyon, France, Chloé came to America with her family to do a road trip in California. She fell in love with California and knew her future belonged there. After finishing her education in Paris and Aix-en-Provence, Chloé came back to the U.S. with a design degree, eager to make a thriving art career. She met Mehdi, a French-Moroccan software engineer, in San Francisco. The couple lived a few years in San Francisco's Mission District, and when Mehdi left his job in San Francisco, they, along with their daughters—four-year-old Lula and twenty-month-old Anouk—decided to take a six-month sabbatical in Mexico. They recently relocated in Los Angeles, and Chloé and Mehdi welcomed me in their new home.

The first thing that stands out when visiting Chloé and Mehdi's home is color! Their light-filled home in the Mar Vista neighborhood embraces the joy of color paired with laid-back California style in every detail. On their travels both to Morocco and Mexico, the family gathered décor elements from their trips and filled their home with souvenirs and objects from their world travels: dream catchers, woven wall art, pompom baskets and totes from Mexico punctuate the decor in almost every room of their home. There are also many of Chloé's designs, like paper flamingo trophies, on the walls.

Although Chloé has now lived more than eight years in the U.S., there are many elements in her lifestyle that have stayed very French: the family always eats dinner together and the kids don't have a special meal; even the youngest gets to try all varieties of food cooked by mom or dad. French is the main language spoken in the household, although four-year-old Lula, who goes to an American school, often tries to use a few English words in the conversation.

The décor of Chloé and Mehdi's interior also features French style: nothing is symmetrical, and the pieces have been chosen without following specific rules of interior design. A colorful midcentury chair sits next to a DIY shelf unit in the dining area. The result is a happy and energetic eclectic interior that feels easy and laid-back.

Chloé confides that her favorite spots in the house are the kids' room and her bedroom, both inundated with natural light.

And then there is the backyard. Since moving here only few months ago, they haven't had the time and budget to furnish the patio area, and Chloé cannot wait to fill it with potted plants. The patio is put to great use, though, with the family enjoying almost every meal, from breakfast to dinner, under the shaded triangles overhanging the outdoor table. The kids spend a great deal of time playing outdoors, which is also reminiscent of the French culture, especially in the South of France.

Although Chloé confides that she's glad to be able to visit family in France during summertime, she feels at home in California and loves her life in Los Angeles. As a guest in their home for one day, I could tell that Chloé and Mehdi have created a good life for themselves. Living as a French family in California sounds like the best of both worlds.

OPPOSITE: Chloé and Mehdi's living room clearly exhibits a global influence: a colorful Moroccan tribal rug sits next to a pink midcentury armchair and an outdoor rattan chair in a striking Majorelle blue.
ABOVE: Mehdi and Anouk enjoy a special dad and daughter moment.

OPPOSITE: Chloé's strong affinity for color is expressed everywhere throughout her house, even in the mixed and matched dining room chairs.

ABOVE: Since they moved very recently to Los Angeles, the couple needed a quick shelving solution for the corner of their dining room. Chloé and Mehdi chose to do a DIY they found online instead of buying something more expensive.

A room to live in: Anouk and Lula's room exhibits bright colors, fun décor elements and lots of easy toy storage options for endless hours of fun and imaginary play. Chloé's paper wall trophies decorate the room.

The family spends most mealtimes and playtime outside, so Chloé's next project will be to create an outdoor room for enjoying more quality time on the patio. For now, the makeshift outdoor dining area is put to great use almost every day.

GRILLED FIG AND BURRATA SALAD

Chloé shares an elegant and delicious salad recipe with grilled figs, prosciutto, and burrata cheese. You can enjoy this dish as a salad or serve it with toasted baguette slices as an appetizer.

SERVES 4

7–10 Mission figs, halved lengthwise

Olive oil

4 handfuls baby arugula salad

8 ounces burrata cheese

4 ounces prosciutto, thinly sliced

Balsamic vinegar

Toasted baguette slices, optional

Salt and pepper

Preheat a grill to medium-high, or use an oven-top plancha.

Brush the sliced figs with olive oil on both sides. Set the figs on the grill or plancha, cut side up, for 2 minutes. Flip them over and cook them for 2 to 3 minutes more, until they get a little brown (be careful to remove them before they get too mushy).

Spread the arugula leaves evenly on a large platter. Distribute the grilled figs evenly on the bed of arugula.

Scoop out the burrata with a teaspoon and place blobs of burrata randomly on the platter.

Pull the prosciutto slices apart and into bite-sized strips. Arrange them on the serving platter.

Drizzle 2 to 3 tablespoons of olive oil and 2 to 3 tablespoons of balsamic vinegar over everything.

Sprinkle with a pinch of salt and black pepper.

Karine + Steve

CAZAUX, BAY OF ARCACHON, FRANCE

KARINE, STEVE AND THEIR DAUGHTER MILA live in Cazaux, a small commune in the bay of Arcachon, a 45-minute-drive from the city of Bordeaux. After a busy and stressful life in London, the family decided to move into their summer home, at first temporarily, and enjoyed the pace of life in this quiet town by the sea so much that the temporary became a long-term situation.

Karine used to own the Bodie and Fou shop in London; she sold it a couple of years ago. At that time, Karine felt burnt out and tired and was looking to recharge her creative batteries. Steve also left a stressful job in finance, and the couple wanted eleven-year-old Mila to experience life in France. There she discovered outdoor sports and developed a passion for skating as well as surfing. She also thrives in gymnastics.

Karine is French and Steve is from New Zealand. They are raising Mila in both French and English languages, and their daughter is completely bilingual. For Karine, it was important that Mila be fluent both in her mother and father tongues.

Mila decorated her room with the help of her mom. Karine did not dictate the design, but worked with her daughter on a room décor mood board, then decorated Mila's space accordingly. Mila is girly as well as being an outdoor sports enthusiast, so her room features both feminine elements and eclectic pieces reflective of her passion for sports.

Karine and Steve's home is a nest. Karine decorated it almost ten years ago, and her style has not aged a bit over time. She wanted her home to feel like a vacation spot, a refuge. Open floor plans, organic materials and linen bedding achieved an overall minimalist feel. She also used strong color statements throughout the house to add some impact into her otherwise white home. The décor elements are eclectic, from Moroccan stools Karine brought back from a recent trip, to Scandinavian pieces she carefully selected.

Nothing is overdone in this home, and every detail shows a strong desire to keep things simple, carefree. The couple spends most time together around the dining table: homework, family talks, meals. This spot is the heart of the home. Karine and Steve's home often has guests, especially Karine's mom, who lives nearby. Karine's sister and niece, Elodie and Lily, regularly take the TGV (high-speed train) from Paris to spend the weekend.

The family always takes breakfasts and dinners together. For them, these moments are priceless and bring the family together. On Sunday mornings, the entire family sits around the dining table, filled with croissants and scrambled eggs, prepared masterfully by Steve, and freshly squeezed orange juice. *"La famille, c'est important"* is a motto in this household. There is even a sign of this saying in the kitchen, a clear reminder that for Karine and Steve, family values are paramount.

The family spends a lot of time in the garden, whether to entertain guests or to take care of the chickens that Karine added to the family backyard a year ago. Steve also built a tree house, but not your typical tree house: it is nested in a tree four meters up from the ground, and carries all the basic necessities for a home office, including WiFi and Internet, so Steve loves to hang out there and watch rugby matches. Karine also occasionally updates her Bodie and Fou blog from the tree house.

And then there is Lulu—Lucas, the Australian Shepard—who runs around the house, indoors and out, following the family's every move and trying to catch the chickens. A happy nest for a happy clan, full of authenticity and warmth.

A reclaimed wooden console serves as a drop-key area in the entryway, while a collection of Moroccan sun hats decorates the wall and adds a global stylishness to the hallway. The tiles are original to the house.

I PROMISE that
SOMEDAY I'll buy you
a place where you
can say "nice VIEW"
& I'll AGREE while
looking straight
AT YOU. x

I'M
THINKING
PLEASE
STAND
BY.

Karine's kitchen has a lived-in feeling. A wall cupboard that hosts all of the dinnerware is decorated with magazine papercuts in bright blue—reminiscent of an ocean house. The opposite wall is painted a dark gunmetal gray to contrast with the all-white canvas of the kitchen and living/dining area.

Mila's room is girly but edgy. Instead of using plastic containers to store personal belongings, Karine chose a set of metal retro-looking travel suitcases. The vintage wooden armoire received a fresh coat of pastel pink paint to give it a modern look.

Karine and Steve's bedroom is minimalist but cozy. The dark gray bed linens add a color accent, and the natural wrinkle of linen gives the room a laid-back but luxurious finish.

Karine and her sister, Elodie, enjoy spending weekends together and letting their daughters, Mila and Lily, create memories and develop a close cousin bond. Lucas, the Australian Shepherd, is never too far away from the family members.

GLUTEN-FREE CHOCOLATE BROWNIES

While brownies are obviously not French, it's the comfort food that Karine loves to bake to unwind and treat her family. She shares this fail-proof brownie-feel-good recipe.

SERVES 8

3 eggs

2 cups (about 200g) sugar

1 ½ cups (200g) cooking chocolate

⅔ cup (about 150g) butter

1 cup gluten-free rice flour

Preheat the oven to 350° F. Line a loaf tin with baking paper.

In a bowl, mix the eggs with the sugar.

In a saucepan, slowly melt the chocolate over low heat, stirring; make sure it doesn't burn. Add the butter to obtain a smooth mix.

Mix the chocolate into the eggs and sugar. Add the flour and combine everything well.

Pour the batter into the loaf tin.

Bake for about 25 to 30 minutes, checking it after 20 minutes and then regularly to see that it cooks through but does not overbake—*et voilà!*

Elodie + Lily

PARIS, FRANCE

ELODIE IS KARINE'S SISTER (Karine + Steve, pages 70–89). She lives in Paris with her thirteen-year-old daughter, Lily. Elodie went through a rough personal time a few years ago, when she and her companion split and work was very demanding. After a few months of darkness and soul searching, Elodie decided to make a huge change in her life and refocus on what really matters to her. She discovered hot yoga and decided to listen to her body and mind. Yoga became a passion, and Elodie is now a certified Bikram yoga instructor by night, while excelling in her day job as a legal and business affairs lawyer.

In her home, Elodie surrounds herself in a minimal mood, refraining from accumulating things and sticking mainly to essentials. The result is a serene, clutter-free abode full of white elements and relaxing décor pieces. When she's not working, Elodie travels extensively with friends all over the French hexagon or reenergizes her spirit with Lily at her sister's in Cazaux, in the Bay of Arcachon.

Elodie is superbly in tune with her body and inner energy. She cut sugar out of her diet after the son of a friend was diagnosed with a condition that prevented him from eating sugar. "I wanted to support him and see what a sugar-free diet would do to my body, says Elodie. Week after week I could feel my body changing and felt more energy throughout the day. I was also sleeping better and felt fully rested in the mornings. My body feels more like a well-oiled machine now. I feel in tune with it, more focused, more positive." Elodie cooks a lot of vegetables at home, which in turn teaches Lily about a balanced diet, but also allows herself and her daughter to indulge in comfort food occasionally, like her delicious tartiflette on page 102.

When they're visiting the family in the Bay of Arcachon, Lily spends extensive time with her cousin, Milla. Lily is constantly surfing, skate boarding and trying new outdoor activities with her cousin. It's important to Elodie and her sister Karine, that the two cousins create a bond and lifelong memories together; the pair of teens even recently traveled with Karine to Bali, Indonesia.

Elodie's 375-square-foot flat in the 17th arrondissement of Paris is small, but her choice of white walls and white painted wooden floors makes it feel quite spacious. She features some apartment's original features, like the gorgeous wooden beams in her living room area, and added some antiques, such as ornate mirrors, to retain the vintage mood.

Lily's room is the largest, and Elodie had a glass window built to maintain the light flow but allow Lily her privacy; white curtains can be used to close the room from general view.

For Elodie, a minimalist and clutter-free interior is an integral part of her journey to higher happiness and personal fulfillment—a clear case of "my home is who I am."

Elodie's immaculate interior is a reflection of her new lifestyle: less house, more home. Her love for natural fibers is defined everywhere in her home: a white linen slipcovered sofa, linen bedding, and storage baskets. Here and there, French thrifted pieces, such as the gilded mirror in the entryway, add a romantic touch to the ensemble.

To allow the light to flow from the living space to Lily's room, Elodie had an industrial-style glass window built. In the past, these types of separations were mainly used in industrial French factory buildings, but the trend is catching up in private interiors.

OPPOSITE: Lily's room is decorated with French vintage thrift finds.

ABOVE: Minimal space, maximum comfort. Elodie's bedroom might be the smallest corner of the apartment, but she managed to create a serene and peaceful space.

TARTIFLETTE

The Tartiflette is a French dish from the Savoy region in the French Alps. It is made of potatoes, Reblochon cheese, lardons, and onions and is usually served in winter, as it is a hearty meal.

SERVES 6 TO 8

8–10 potatoes

3 cups diced non-smoked lardons*

1 onion, diced (optional)

2 ½ cups crème fraîche

Pepper

Salt

1 full Reblochon-style cheese
or similar soft cheese

* Alternatively use bacon or pancetta.

** Reblochon is a semi-soft, fondue-type cheese. Thin slices of Brie or Camembert can be substituted.

Preheat the oven at 350° F. Prepare a dish for baking.

Peel the potatoes and boil them until they are soft.

In a frying pan over medium heat, place two spoons of olive oil and cook the lardons (or bacon or pancetta) and onion. Once cooked, add the crème fraîche and mix thoroughly; [reduce heat to low or turn off heat at this point?]

Cut the boiled potatoes into small squares and add them to the mixture. Let them sit for 20 to 30 minutes so they marinate in the bacon/onion/cream mixture. Add pepper to taste (the more, the better) and salt if needed. Transfer the mixture to an oven dish.

Slice the Reblochon cheese in half; remove the crust from the top, bottom, and sides. Spread the Reblochon on the top of the potatoes.

Bake for 45 minutes to 1 hour. The dish is ready when the cheese is golden, crispy, and bubbling.

Serve with a vinaigrette green salad.

Claire + Karim

RABAT, MOROCCO

CLAIRE AND KARIM, a French-Moroccan couple, relocated to France in 2010. They kept their home in Rabat, Morocco, as a place to escape the crazy pace of work: Karim is an entrepreneur in the bakery business and works long hours. Whenever their kids—Hayat, sixteen, and Hicham, seventeen—have school breaks, the family hops on a two-hour flight to enjoy a slow pace in Morocco.

Claire wanted this home to feel like a vacation spot. She didn't decorate in a hurry but took her time finding pieces and furniture that would work together without following strict rules: Scandinavian furniture lives happily next to industrial flea finds and Moroccan tribal rugs. Claire was particular about one thing, though—the use of color. She applied color on some accent walls throughout the house to contrast with the white walls. She also added color through her furniture and wall art. Claire likes to mix and match her décor elements and despises "total look" interiors. For her, décor is a very personal business, and she wants her house to look and feel like her, not like it came out of a magazine.

When she's not bringing back or shipping pieces she has found in Paris, Claire works with local craftsmen to design pieces for her home: the wall bookcase and outdoor sofa set were handmade by a local woodworker, and a few of her outdoor metal furniture pieces were handmade by a blacksmith. It's important for Claire to embrace Karim and her kids' Moroccan cultural heritage in her interior. Even though the ensemble looks overall European, there are touches of Moroccan craft and art everywhere: the low coffee table in the living room is actually an old Moroccan door sitting on casters.

Claire and Karim remodeled the house entirely: volume was added by extending the ceiling heights; an oak parquet floor was installed throughout the home; and the couple deliberately chose to open the house to the outdoors: in every room there is easy access to the lush and luxurious garden.

Hosting dinners is something the couple loves to do when at their summer home. Hanging out on the patio with a bottle of wine and a homemade dinner is a great way to catch up with friends they left when they relocated to France. Hayat and Hicham have also kept in touch with many of their school friends, so the house is, naturally, a favorite spot to hang out by the pool or enjoy a homemade chocolate cake or Moroccan crêpes prepared by Fatima, the longtime cook and superintendent of the house while the family is away.

The family enjoys sports activities here: running, walking their two German Shepherds, golfing, playing tennis, and taking surf lessons at the beach. Life is good in this home, free of stress; and then it's time to get back to the real world and the gray Paris weather, until the next holiday break and escape to paradise.

In her open floor plan kitchen, Claire played with industrial details and modern elements, adding a splash of vibrant tangerine. The ethnic Berber rug makes the transition between entryway and kitchen.

The reading area mixes wonderful Scandinavian lines with a global style, thanks to the use of a Beni Ouarain black and white tribal rug.

Modern details in the kitchen include functional objects as display pieces, while a spacious white cabinet hides the cooking appliances.

In the master bedroom, which opens to the outdoors, Claire and Karim mixed industrial pieces with Scandinavian design. Another rug adds some global flair and serves as a reminder of this family's cultural heritage.

Hicham chose a blue palette for his bedroom. By his bed, a vintage flag reflects of his fascination with America. His dream is to go to the U.S. to pursue his education.

Hayat's room, with its striking turquoise wall, has a more feminine mood. A mezzanine was added to use all of the ceiling's height and serves as a private area for the teen.

Claire and Karim's home is open to the outdoors. The couple hosts a lot of get-togethers with friends when they are vacationing in Morocco. During the hot days, teens, guests and dogs freely move from the outdoors to inside the house to avoid the aggressive North African sun.

CREAMY ZUCCHINI SOUP

This delicious soup is packed with flavor, thanks to shallots and herbs de Provence.

SERVES 4

5-7 zucchinis

1 small onion or shallot

1 tablespoon of olive oil

Herbs de Provence for seasoning

Salt and pepper

2 ½ cups water

2 tablespoons cream cheese or Boursin garlic and fine herbs cheese

Bread crumbs, toasted baguette slices, or Parmesan crisps, for garnish

Peel and cut the zucchinis into tiny slices.

Cut the onion or shallot into small pieces.

In a medium-size soup pan over medium heat, cook the onion/shallot and zucchini in a little bit of oil for 10 minutes. Add herbes de Provence, salt, and pepper to taste.

Transfer the mixture into a blender and add the water. Blend until the mixture is liquefied, smooth and crumble-free.

Transfer liquid back into a soup pan and cook over a low heat. When hot but not boiling, add the cream cheese/Boursin and let the mixture reduce to thicken to your liking, stirring frequently.

Garnish each bowl of soup with bread crumbs, a toasted baguette slice, or a Parmesan crisp.

Charlotte + Maxime

PARIS, FRANCE

CHARLOTTE AND MAXIME are the charismatic duo behind Selency by Brocante Lab, a successful start-up specializing in secondhand furniture and décor items. Both in their late twenties, they are the poster couple for success.

Charlotte studied marketing and landed a job in a big Paris-based cosmetics corporation for a few years. She then felt that a smaller structure would be a better fit for her and joined a company as a project manager. Three years later, and with a whole lot more expertise under her belt, she decided to start her own business. What field, though? Charlotte wanted a job where she wouldn't count the hours because she would be living her passion: "Choose a job you love, and you will never have to work a day in your life," said Confucius.

Quickly, Charlotte identified that décor and vintage were her calling; after all, she had grown up with a mother who loved vintage and took her to flea markets and antique shops throughout her childhood. She had even done a summer internship as a teenager and now remembered how incredibly fascinating this field was: every piece had a story to tell.

Charlotte launched her company, Selency by Brocante Lab, and Maxime joined as a partner soon after. After two and half years in business, Selency has become a successful platform connecting antique sellers and vintage buyers, with more than 30 employees and 1,400 antique sellers referenced.

Charlotte and Maxime's interior and design choices reflect their passion for antiquing. For Charlotte, it's much more interesting to scout a vintage find than to buy mass market furniture—plus the resell value of an antique piece makes it easy to change your décor. Her design choices are all about intuition, and tests and trials. She confides that her style in décor is to choose one strong object and then work around it. Sometimes the strategy fails and sometimes it works wonderfully. She recently bought a vintage green velvet sofa and added accessories to suit—or sometimes contrast with—this piece.

"Decorating our home is just like choosing our fashion: we all have our own individual style, and interior design is a personal business. The furniture and furnishings you choose have to fit your lifestyle. If you host a lot of dinners, then you need a special spot in your house for your gathering table. If you are more of a couch potato, then invest in a good sofa or lounging chair," says Charlotte.

Charlotte and Maxime love to host dinners in their Parisian apartment, and Charlotte takes great pleasure in cooking for friends. So the couple saved to acquire their dream piece: a vintage marble-top Tulip table. Because they didn't want to go for a total look with the

expected matching Tulip chairs, they opted for caned vintage chairs that complement their newly acquired table wonderfully. Charlotte believes in *coup de cœur* in decoration, or love at first sight. "Experiment, take risks, find what works and what doesn't work for you!" she says. "We're not in the '50s anymore, where your décor has to stay the same over the years. Décor has to evolve with you."

Charlotte and Maxime's apartment, in the 18th arrondissement of Paris, is filled with story-telling pieces, and if you were to visit them in a year, chances are the furniture would probably have changed or been relocated throughout their flat. Because for them, décor needs to evolve as you grow personally. In any case, I have a feeling that if I were to go visit the pair again, I'd have another big *coup de cœur!*

Charlotte surrounds herself with items and décor elements that have meaning to her, but she's never afraid to move pieces around in her apartment.

One rule to decorating the French way is to follow no rules. Here a vintage rattan chair happily coexists with a midcentury floor lamp and a thrifted scale.

OPPOSITE: A vintage green sofa gets a modern update with a colorful pillow.

A small but mighty, typically Parisian kitchen is proof that big meals can be prepared in a tiny space.
OPPOSITE: Charlotte's expert eye thrifted this Danish sideboard and vintage suitcases, which are used to store objects discreetly.

The art of mixing and matching is quintessentially French: a tulip table is surrounded by Bauhaus-era caned chairs for a laid-back dining area.

A French Crapaud armchair sits next to a modern Swedish metal cabinet and a vintage gilded mirror. OPPOSITE: Charlotte and Maxime's bedroom is the only room that received a colored wall treatment. A soft shade of green brings the perfect amount of calm and Zen effect to the room.

MUSHROOM RISOTTO

Originating in Italy, risotto is a rice dish cooked in broth to a creamy consistency. Charlotte recommends serving it with an arugula salad for a flavorful and chic but easy meal.

SERVES 6

1 ½ cups mixed mushrooms

½ cup chopped parsley

2 cups water

1 chicken bouillon cube

1 tablespoon olive oil

2 shallots, minced

2 garlic cloves, minced

1 ½ cups risotto rice

½ glass white wine

1 cup crème fraîche

⅓ cup grated Parmesan

Salt and pepper

Clean the mushrooms and cut them roughly into pieces.

Heat a pan and cook the mushrooms for a few minutes. Add some chopped parsley when the mushrooms are cooked and set aside.

In a large pot, bring the water and bouillon cube to the boil to make broth.

In the pan used to cook mushrooms, heat the olive oil over medium heat and cook the minced shallot and garlic for 1 minute. Add the risotto rice and stir until the rice is translucent, about 3 minutes.

Add the wine and keep stirring. Then gradually add the broth, one ladle at a time. When the liquid has been absorbed by the rice, keep adding the broth ladle after ladle, until the rice is cooked. You might not need to use all the liquid. When the rice is cooked, add the crème fraîche and Parmesan and keep stirring.

Add the mushroom/parsley mixture and season to taste with salt and pepper.

It is ready to serve when the rice has a creamy consistency.

Annouchka + David

ANNOUCHKA, DAVID, and their two-year-old daughter Chloé live in the quaint neighborhood of Pacific Heights in San Francisco, California. After ten years in New York City, the couple decided to relocate to California to enjoy a more laid-back lifestyle and start a family.

Annouchka and David met when they were living in Montréal; she is French-Swiss from her mother's side and Canadian from her dad's, while David is Canadian. French is the spoken language in the household, although Annouchka confesses that English words come out in the French conversations: "Sometimes," she says,

141

"you need two words in English for a whole sentence in French." However, the couple makes it a point to speak only in French with Chloé, who will attend the French school in San Francisco, beginning with kindergarten. Marlowe, the family poodle, also speaks Frenglish, answering to commands in both languages.

Annouchka is an interior designer; she has her own company, J'adore Decore, and is busy with clients' projects. Her approach to interior design is very organic. Instead of the one-size-fits-all approach to designing a space, she helps decorate her clients' homes as Europeans do, creating a home that fits the style of his occupants, and not designing to impress the guests or "keep up with the Joneses."

Similarly, for her own home, Annouchka wanted her interior to feel personal. "I didn't want my home to be like everyone else's," she says. She kept a lot of family estate pieces—like an antique table in her living room and her grandmother's Louis Vuitton trunk—rearranged furniture that moved with them from their New York home, and brought back carefully curated finds from the couple's trips abroad. "Instead of adding décor elements from a one-stop shopping trip, I think it's much more interesting to bring back objects from travels; they remind you of your travels and add something unique and offbeat to one's interior," advises Annouchka.

As an avid reader, David wanted to have a reading room. So Annouchka used the parlor area to create a quiet reading retreat filled with built-in bookcases, and she scouted some antique chairs during a trip to London. The media room has become a playroom, allowing Annouchka to monitor Chloé's playtime while preparing meals in the kitchen. "Since we moved into this house in 2014, it has changed considerably, evolving with us and our needs and tastes," adds Annouchka.

Chloé eats before her parents because she goes to bed around 7:30; then Annouchka and David enjoy some quiet time together. Chloe eats the same food as her parents, usually the leftovers from her parents' previous dinner. It's important for Annouchka and David to develop Chloé's palate early on, because they plan on traveling again once the kids are a bit older. "We used to travel a lot, even when Chloé was a baby," Annouchka confesses, "but we're taking a break, with baby number two coming. Traveling with young kids takes a big organization, and we were used to traveling with only carry-on bags. We look forward to traveling again as a family, though," says Annouchka.

When asked what she kept from her European cultural roots while living in North America, Annouchka confesses that she's always felt European at heart. "Our education, our critical reasoning, our passion for heated debates, our way of seeing and enjoying life—these things never disappear, even if you spend a lifetime away from your native culture," she responds.

Chevron-pattern wooden floors add
a Parisian flair to this San Francisco
Victorian home.
OPPOSITE: Annouchka's spacious
kitchen opens up to the play area
designed for Chloé..

Vintage and antique elements, like this wooden dresser, bring French character to the dining area.

Annouchka chose a few different graphic wallpapers for her home, like this gorgeous oversized flower wallpaper on the stairs. OPPOSITE: She had already purchased the dining chair fabric as a *coup de cœur, so* when she scouted these vintage formal dining chairs, she knew she had found the perfect fit for her marbled pink fabric.

This is Chloé's new room. Annouchka recently relocated it here to make room for baby number two, who will use Chloé's former room. With the growing family, decorating is always a work in progress.

In her bedroom, Annouchka added some extra-long linen window treatments, with an eight-plus-inch hem. "The fabric store double-checked many times if I was sure I wanted the linens that long," Annouchka recalls. "In France, we love for the curtains to fall naturally on the floor."

OPPOSITE: A work in progress in baby number two's room, and another beautiful and unique feather wallpaper covering.

ABOVE: In her bedroom, Annouchka keeps her jewelry at view using a Buddha sculpture. It's the personal touches that add a character to a space.

CLAFOUTIS

A clafoutis is a baked French dessert of fruit, traditionally black cherries or berries, arranged in a buttered dish and covered with a thick flan-like batter. Annouchka's clafoutis is dairy-free, but it can be made with dairy products, as discussed in the footnote.

SERVES 6

5 eggs

³/₄ cup coconut sugar

¹/₂ cup flour

1 pinch of salt

³/₄ cup of unsweetened vanilla almond milk*

2 tablespoons melted and cooled dairy-free butter*

1 cup of coconut cream*

2 tablespoons of Grand Marnier liqueur

1 ¹/₂ packages frozen unsweetened mixed berries, thawed halfway

* If you are not making this recipe dairy-free, 2% milk, regular butter, and whipping cream are fine substitutions.

Preheat the oven to 375° F. Butter a large glass pie dish.

In the jar of a blender, put the eggs, sugar, flour, salt, almond milk, and butter; blend well (about 30 seconds). Then add the cream and liqueur and blend again for about 20 seconds.

Place the berries in the bottom of the pie dish. Then pour the blended mixture on top.

Bake for about 40 minutes, or until puffy and golden. You can also test for doneness by inserting a knife in the middle; if it comes out clean, the clafoutis is done.

Let cool completely at room temperature before eating. Clafoutis is even better the second day.

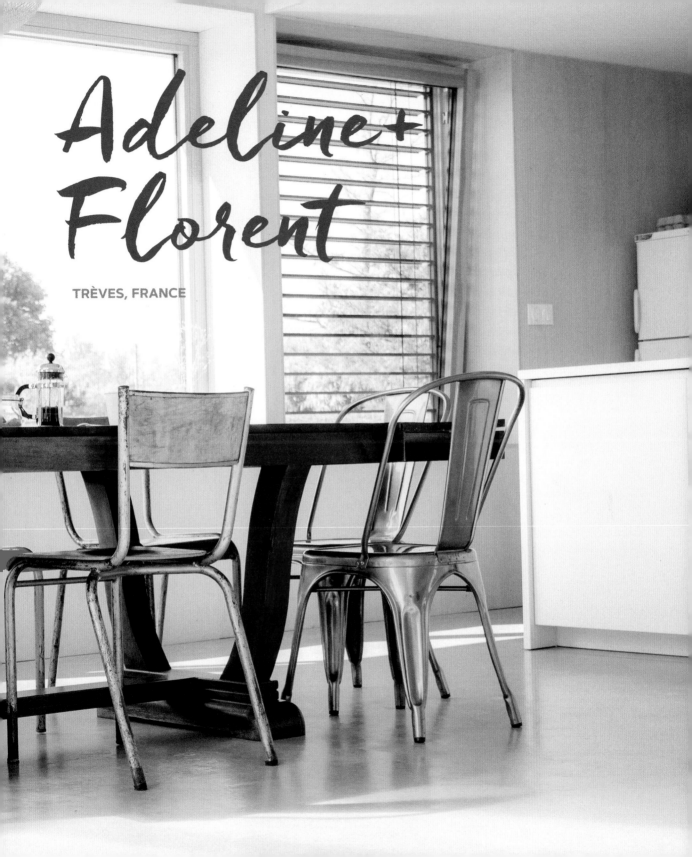

Adeline + Florent

TRÈVES, FRANCE

ADELINE AND FLORENT live in a little village called Trèves, in the Lyon region. They met while studying at the university in Lyon, and after a life in the city decided to make a profound change. Florent took the family business and has become an organic farmer. Adeline is a graphic designer and stylist; she works with famous French brands as well as styling window displays for stores in Lyon.

Adeline and Florent built their own house. They wanted a modern farm on the family property and managed to execute the project with limited costs, and under budget. Their home—a big, modern wooden structure with lots of windows that oversee valleys and pastures—stands out as you approach the tiny country road.

Adeline and Florent have two kids, Ninon, five, and Melville, nine. For the couple, offering a quality of life to their children, away from the city and the busy world, was a profound wish. When both kids come home from the local school, they play in the fields, help their dad on the farm, or visit their grandmother and aunt who live nearby. On weekends the family escapes to Lyon to visit museums and get their fix of city living; Adeline and Florent feel it's important for their children to learn about art and culture.

Food is an important part of the children's education, especially with an organic farmer dad. Adeline and the kids grow a garden so the kids understand that what goes on the plate grew from the soil. Melville takes great pride in caring for the family's chicken coop.

Adeline has a natural eye for décor. Her home is filled with flea markets finds, collected items and family inherited furniture. Her favorite piece is her grandmother's farm table, the *pièce d'honneur* in the main family room; the table was acquired by her grandmother from the church that welcomed her as a refugee when she and her family fled Cambodia.

If Adeline has to pick a new piece to decorate her home, she always checks whether there is a flea find that would suit her needs. As a result, the family's home has a unique character, with its wooden walls from floor to ceiling, cement floors, and bits and pieces of collected items. The house looks a lot more spacious than its actual 1,350-square-foot size. The most striking thing about Adeline and Florent's home is that they do not decorate to impress the visitor or to keep up with trends, but rather try to surround themselves with pieces that have a meaning for their life and their kids'.

Adeline loves to surround herself with plants, so her living room also serves as a plant nursery and also teaches the kids about patience with nature. There is definitely a Zen feel and calmness in this family's home or while spending time chatting with Adeline and Florent, along with a holistic approach to life, family values and the love of mother nature.

The mezzanine overlooks the living space and was furnished with low-height makeshift shelves that now display Melville and Ninon's books and board game collection. A Moroccan rug and midcentury rocker complete the eclectic look of this corner.

A modern sofa faces the floor-to-ceiling windows, and a few vintage pieces scouted by Adeline add a warm touch to the living space. The plywood walls and concrete floors add an organic and modern texture to the interior.

Adeline's plant nursery collection, displayed on a vintage bench, instantly adds an urban-jungle effect to the living room.

Melville's room features a pale blue palette. Painted "feet" on the vintage thrifted chair's legs add a fun and modern twist.

Ninon's room stylishly embraces childhood with pretend-play sets and colorful details. Adeline cleverly used two crib mattresses to create a reading/napping area for Ninon. Recycling and repurposing furniture and décor elements allow Adeline and Florent to avoid overconsuming, especially on pieces that will quickly become obsolete as their children grow.

GRATIN DAUPHINOIS

The gratin dauphinois is a traditional regional French dish made of potatoes and cream, from the historic Dauphiné region in south-east France.

SERVES 4

7–8 medium-sized potatoes

3 garlic cloves, pressed or minced

1 teaspoon herbes de Provence

Salt and pepper

½ cup milk

2 cups heavy cream

Nutmeg, grated or ground

Preheat the oven at 350° F.

Peel the potatoes and rinse them; cut into slices. Arrange slices in an oven dish.

Add the garlic, herbes de Provence, and salt and pepper to taste.

Pour the milk and heavy cream over the potatoes. The potatoes should be almost covered by the liquid. Sprinkle lightly with nutmeg.

Bake for about 1 hour to 1 ½ hours. The gratin is ready when all the liquid has reduced and the gratin is bubbling and golden on top. Serve immediately, although it is also delicious reheated the next day.

Anne-Sophie + Pierre

LILLE, FRANCE

Anne-Sophie used a space next to the modern chimney to display her cherished collection of midcentury objects.

ANNE-SOPHIE AND PIERRE met when they were both working in an advertising agency a few moons ago. Both graphic designers, they share a natural eye for beauty and design. When they decided to acquire a new home in Lille, they drew the plan for their dream house and had an architect bring the project to life. They now live in it and have filled it with curated pieces from their favorite era and style: midcentury modern.

Anne-Sophie and Pierre welcomed their daughter, Nell, twelve years ago. Her arrival signaled a deep need for change, and the couple decided that their lifestyle of over-working needed to dramatically shift for them to enjoy a good quality of life. Anne-Sophie quit her time-consuming job in advertising to work from home in her new interior design studio, So-Deco. She now consults with clients who want to change their interiors. Pierre, who had founded his own ad/marketing agency, sold his shares to his founding partners and recon-nected with his original passion: design. He now creates décor pieces—for instance, lamps—which he self-markets under the ByPan! brand.

In their home, Anne-Sophie and Pierre surrounded themselves with décor elements and thrifted pieces they have carefully selected. They love to flea and find unique midcentury furnishings. "My favorite piece in our home is the Eames Molded Plywood lounge chair; I love its timeless, simple line. It hasn't aged a bit since its creation in 1946!" says Pierre. When it comes to purchasing furniture, both Anne-Sophie and Pierre have to agree on what is brought into the house.

Twelve-year-old Nell is surprisingly design-alert for her age. She has been accompanying her parents to flea markets since she was young, and Anne-Sophie confides that for her and Pierre, it's important to train Nell's eyes for design; they often visit museums to encourage her to develop design sensitivity.

The sense of family bond is very strong in this household. The family eats breakfast together every morning and shares dinnertime together as well. Nell is now in middle school, and Anne-Sophie drives her and picks her up every day; on the way home and at snack time, the two talk a lot about Nell's day at school, and Anne-Sophie helps her daughter with her homework. Anne-Sophie's parenting approach to help Nell is to develop her self-confidence and let her "grow" without pressure. "I don't want her to feel that she has to fit the mold, to try to be someone she's not because that's what is expected of her by society. I want to help her reach her own maximum capaci-ties and feel good about her achievements," confides Anne-Sophie. "Nell is blossoming in front of our very eyes into a strong and self-confident young adult."

This philosophy of slow life and self-acceptance is translated in the interior style of this family home. Anne-Sophie and Pierre's home is a cocoon, a nest, where the family's values are cherished: listening, supporting and respecting each other, making family moments matter. Because they designed their own dream house, the flow in the house is natural, the pieces collected seem to be placed in exactly the right spot, almost as if they miraculously found their natural spot in the home. This family and their home are the epitome of the Danish notion of *hygge*—the philosophy of enjoying life's simple pleasures, family, graciousness, contentment and good feelings.

Vibrant graphic-print pillows complement the vintage wooden chairs collected by Anne-Sophie and Pierre.

Anne-Sophie and Pierre share their workspace together, a career choice they made when they welcomed their daughter Nell. Working together from home allows them to have lunch together when Nell is at school.

Vintage shelves display a collection of
midcentury objects, and below is an
original Apple Macintosh.

In her master bedroom, Anne-Sophie followed some feng shui guidelines: a photo of Pierre and her is displayed above the bed, and the bedroom exhibits a neutral palette and mood.

OPPOSITE: Anne-Sophie tries to surround herself with meaningful pieces in her bedroom. A collection of books, art and vintage miniature cars enhance the room's soft, calm color scheme.

In the North of France, the timid sunshine is always welcome, and this terrace on the main living floor of the house is a great relaxing spot under the northern sun.

LENTIL SALAD

Here is a super-simple recipe that Anne-Sophie loves to prepare for her family.

SERVES 3

2 cups green lentils, sorted

6 cups broth or water

Seasonings of your choice,
    such as herbes de Provence

3 garlic cloves, minced

½ cup of chopped parsley

3 tablespoons olive oil

1 tablespoon balsamic vinegar

Salt and pepper

½ cup of shaved Parmesan

Poached eggs (1 per serving)

In a medium-size pan, place the lentils with the broth or water and seasonings of your choice. With the lid on, bring to a boil and then reduce to a simmer and cook until tender, about 15 to 20 minutes. Let lentils cool down.

In a bowl, combine the lentils, garlic, parsley, olive oil, and vinegar. Season with salt and pepper to taste. Mix well. Add the shaved Parmesan.

Spoon into individual portions and add the poached egg on top.

Jessica + Vincent

BORDEAUX, FRANCE

JESSICA AND VINCENT live in the beautiful city of Bordeaux with two-year-old daughter Olympe. They moved two years ago, after living in a small village near Montpellier. When Jessica was pregnant, she felt the need to go back home where she grew up and her family still lives. "It was important for me to get closer to my family for support as a new mom, and to raise my daughter in my native region," confides Jessica. Jessica owns a successful interior design company, BOH, which caters to the hospitality industry. She's also in the process of creating an event rental business.

For her new apartment in Bordeaux, she completely changed the décor from the vintage industrial style of her loft in the Montpellier area. "Each home calls for its own style," says Jessica, who feels that the current flat, inundated with natural light, needed a more contemporary look and vibe. "Because we have so much light, I wanted to add color accents and gradually added pieces that inspired me."

There is no formal recipe in the way Jessica decorates her home. In contrast to her job, where decorating a hotel or a bed and breakfast is dictated by clients' requirements and stricter rules of interior design, decorating her own home was more a labor of love for Jessica. She kept a few pieces from the old house, like the industrial-style dining table, but added flea finds and contemporary elements.

Jessica and Vincent travel a lot around the globe, and they love to bring back treasures from their trips to Bali, India or Gabon to decorate their space. These curated elements, from mixed and matched eras and locations, bring an authenticity to the interior. Jessica mentions that she despises total look interiors. While she is the decorator and makes decisions about the décor, Vincent validates or vetoes her choices. "I mostly agree, but sometimes, I have to put my veto. I have to stop Jessica when we go to flea markets, for example, because she wants to buy everything on impulse, especially vintage chairs." Vincent's favorite room in the house is their living room, where the family spends most of their time. He also cherishes the collection of tribal masks they brought back from a market in Libreville, Gabon.

Jessica is very attached to her artwork: she used to manage the gallery collection of a contemporary art museum, so art holds a special place in her art. When asked what piece in her interior she couldn't separate from, she replies "If there was a fire and I had to save something, I'd grab my wall art. No, scratch that! I'd run to my closet to get my grandmother's collection of vintage ball gowns. This is irreplaceable!"

When they are not working, Jessica and Vincent enjoy receiving friends and cooking meals. Jessica loves to cook. She says that for her, cooking is an act of love. "You're not just feeding people; you show them how much they matter to you." The house has a no-invitation-necessary policy.

"My friends are like family," Jessica says. "They know they can stop by at any time in my house." And when they do, a quick happy hour or meal is crafted for the occasion.

Food is definitely an important part of Jessica and Vincent's life. While Saturdays are dedicated to walks around the city and its parks or hanging out with a picnic at the beach with Olympe and Rym—Vincent's eight-year-old daughter from a previous union, who comes two weekends a month and on school breaks to stay with her dad—or grabbing some white wine and oyster trays at the local shack, Sundays are reserved for hanging out with family and food. If the couple is not at the weekly farmers market tasting organic foods, they host family meals that can last for hours.

Meanwhile, little Olympe is learning the importance of food in the process. Breakfast and dinners are spent and enjoyed together, and Olympe eats the same meal as her parents. Food sharing is definitely an important value in this household. Jessica's parents are wine negotiators in the Bordeaux region, so the love of good food and good wine runs in the family and has been passed on from generation to generation.

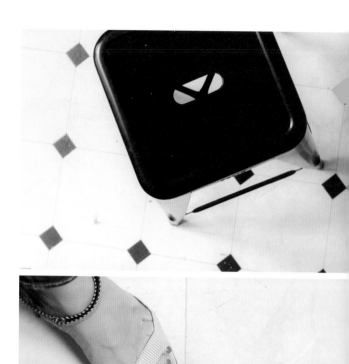

Jessica's kitchen is small, but that's where all of her magic cooking happens. The large window filters the perfect amount of light, and the vintage-look floor tiles add an authentic French charm to this kitchen.

A vintage industrial dining table is surrounded by vintage chairs: Jessica is described by Vincent as an antique chair addict! Behind the table, a French vintage rolling bar cart displays a collection of beverages for the next get-together with friends and family.

Jessica often reads stories to Olympe to encourage her imagination and hopefully develop her love for reading. OPPOSITE: The pink sofa doubles as a bed when Rym, Vincent's daughter from a previous union, comes to visit her dad.

Olympe's room has many romantic details, including a beautiful leaf wallpaper by the crib. The color palette was deliberately kept soft and gives a retro charm to this toddler's room.

Jessica and Vincent's bedroom features a striking white and blue accent wallpaper and is minimally decorated with luxurious textures and vintage elements, like this antique dresser.

WHITE SANGRIA

Jessica and Vincent put their vintage bar cart to great use entertaining friends at home. Here is a fresh, summery cocktail recipe that is a feast to the eyes and palate.

SERVES 4

1 bottle Sauvignon Blanc or other dry white wine

2 cups Saint Germain French liqueur

1 peach, cut into small cubes

6 strawberries, cut into small bites

6 raspberries, cut into small bites

Stir the wine and liqueur in a carafe and add the cut fruits.

Let the mix marinate in the refrigerator for up to 6 hours before serving.

Serve in ice-filled glasses. Cheers!

Loanah + Romain

ANGOULÊME, FRANCE

LOANAH AND ROMAIN live in Angoulême, in southwestern France, with their five-year-old son, Jules. They moved here four years ago, after living in Bordeaux. Loanah's family is originally from Angoulême, and her grandmother lives in the neighborhood.

Romain is an *ébéniste,* or wood worker, by trade, and after renovating a few houses in Bordeaux and playing house-flippers, the couple decided to open their own furniture and design shop, Blomkål, and move into this 1930s single-story home. While walking with her family in the neighborhood, Loanah recalls, she spotted this house for sale and "saw it as a sign."

The couple didn't remodel this house extensively, as they had done with their flip houses; they wanted to keep the original features and charm of this old house. They refreshed the paint on the walls and renovated the top part of the garage to serve as a guest room: Romain's brother, Bastien, also works at Blomkål and often stops by for the night to avoid a long commute. The extra sleeping space is also used for frequent summer guests. .

Loanah has filled her home with objects she cherishes. She used to flea market a lot and grew attached to some of the pieces she scouted. She loves displaying her finds with unexpected elements and follows her intuition when it comes to decorating her home. Some Blomkål prototypes or collection samples make it into their home as well. The result is an eclectic space filled with personality, where antiques happily coexist with more contemporary elements.

And then there is Jules's room. While it is chic, it is comfortably adapted to a five-year-old. Romain placed a wallpaper from French brand Kisikol above Jules's bed area, and all of Jules's toys add more pops of color. A big green chalkboard is filled with notes, messages and masks, and Loanah created a desk corner for Jules.

Blomkål is the "second child" of Loanah and Romain. The brand proudly designs "Made in France" furniture and décor pieces from the family workshop: pure, simple lines drawn out on light wood paneling, combined with subtle colors, plywood, or cork. Blomkål products are engaging and authentic, with a lot of customizable pieces: for instance, a coffee table can become a dinner table with adaptable and interchangeable feet.

Loanah and Romain love relaxing at home. They have a loyal group of friends who love to cook together and prepare simple dishes. In the summer months, Loanah and Romain spend their days outside on the adorable patio they set up. Loanah admits that the garden becomes literally an extra room for the house.

Loanah's favorite room in the house is her kitchen. "I never cook formal recipes; I randomly experiment with ingredients. Whether it's last-minute tapas platters or more complicated dishes, entertaining is all about sharing a good time with people you care about."

ABOVE: A vintage coat rack in Loanah and Romain's entryway hosts a collection of hats and fashion accessories. The blue painted door and moldings add a vintage charm to this tiny space.

OPPOSITE: The family—as well as Eden, the not-so-camera-shy French bulldog—spends an extensive amount of time on their patio during the warm seasons. A fabric triangle canopy offers protection from sunrays and poetically dances with the wind.

OPPOSITE: Loanah and Romain's living room is eclectic, with a tan leather sofa and a vintage wooden printer's drawer cabinet.

ABOVE: A clever and original way to display décor objects: wooden wine crates are arranged on the wall to display Loanah's favorite pieces.

The kitchen has a shabby and romantic feel with lots of thrifted French vintage finds, such as the butcher's weighing scale and the wooden workshop table. Some modern elements, like white metal stools, help modernize the ensemble.

PREVIOUS OVERLEAF: Jules's eye candy room is stylish and elegant while still embracing childhood, thanks to the use of strong color statements. For his bed, Loanah chose French linen bedding and pillows, and Romain placed a colorful strip of French brand wallpaper as a headboard. Loanah also arranged a desk area for Jules using scouted vintage finds such as an antique French elementary school desk and industrial factory metal bins to store small toys. She completed the look with a nostalgic green chalkboard wall. Original-era building elements such as the marble chimney add an authentic retro charm to the room.

RIGHT: The guest quarters, in a space above the garage, was reorganized to host friends and family who want to sleep over. Simple, natural textures and wooden walls are reminiscent of Romain's woodworking background.

OPPOSITE: Loanah and Romain's all-white bedroom is filled with French antiques and embraces a romantic French mood.

This guest room was designed by Romain—a woodworker by trade—and Loanah added her personal touches, like painting the headboard area with a house shape. Here is proof that experimenting in your personal décor pays off!

PASTA CARBONARA

Pasta Carbonara is a classic comfort food dish, but Loanah's carbonara has a unique Savora mustard French flavor.

SERVES 4

Pasta (we use linguine)

1 red onion, minced

1 tablespoon olive oil

1 ½ cups Pancetta or bacon, cut into small pieces

8 ounces crème fraîche or sour cream

1 tablespoon Savora mustard (available online, or substitute American mustard)

Salt and pepper

1 cup grated Comté cheese or Parmesan, plus extra for garnish

Cook the pasta according to package directions.

Meanwhile, in a stovetop pan, cook the onion in the olive oil.

Add the bacon or pancetta and let it cook with the onion until crispy.

Add the crème fraîche, mustard, and salt and pepper to taste.

Add the cheese and stir until blended.

Drain the pasta when cooked, and serve it with the sauce on top, garnished with some grated cheese.

Selwa + Ryan

SELWA IS FRENCH-MOROCCAN and Ryan is American. They live in Herndon, Virginia, in the Washington, DC, area, with their two-year-old daughter Kira. Selwa has lived in France—she studied in Paris and Bordeaux—the Netherlands and Spain before moving to the United States in 2001. Ryan is originally from Pennsylvania.

Selwa and Ryan started a remodeling company, specializing in bathrooms and kitchens. Selwa takes care of client interactions—estimates, design input and invoicing—and Ryan handles and supervises the work crews and construction sites.

In their 1,800-square-foot home, the couple used their knowledge as trade insiders to remodel their interior: they opened the space to allow for better flow; they fully remodeled the kitchen and all bathrooms; and they installed a new brushed, wide-plank oak floor throughout the main and top floors.

Selwa's style is eclectic, with lots of Scandinavian elements living happily with vintage and industrial finds. There are no rules for her interior choices: if it works with the current décor and it serves a real purpose, it makes the

cut; if not, it's out. Selwa is very intuitive in her approach to decorating.

With the arrival of Kira, the family had to update their interior and move things around (or hide things) from the curious toddler. Kira has a dedicated play space in the living room, so her parents can monitor her activities when they are in the kitchen or the main room. While Mom or Dad is busy cooking a meal in the kitchen, Kira imitates and plays in her pretend kitchen, baking cookies and cupcakes for the family or her dolls. It's hours of endless play and fun.

Kira speaks French with her mom and English with her dad. Ryan has always wished to learn French, and while he understands a lot of it, he is not yet fluent. Somehow, Kira has adapted to this situation and instinctively switches from one language to another. At daycare, one of Kira's favorite caretakers is Hispanic, so Kira is learning some Spanish words as well; she says *"agua"* when she wants someone to serve her a glass of water, or *"no mas"* when she's full. It's pretty hilarious to see how this tiny human adapts to the spoken languages in her environment.

Selwa and Ryan's style of parenting tends toward the French European: it is all about adventures and experiences in their approach to raising Kira. They want her to be curious, to try things, to learn by trials and mistakes, to experience everything by herself—as long as she's not in harm's way. The French and Europeans in general embrace a sensory and hands-on learning philosophy: "If it hurts, don't do it again." Of course, with close monitoring so that the child is never in real danger.

Kira's room is the jewel of the house: a tent has been installed in her room so that bedtime storytelling takes place in a magical spot. Dad or mom sits with her under the tent, dim lights are turned on, and Kira is transported into the story. Selwa and Ryan also try to teach Kira to play by herself and develop her imagination. They don't want to her to fall into an "only child" attention-seeking pattern where she would always need a parent to play with or entertain her.

Kira eats exactly what mom and dad eat. Every night the family sits together and enjoys a homemade meal. Selwa and Ryan participate in a Community Supported Agriculture program, receiving a crate of organic crops every week from a nearby farm. It forces Selwa to experiment with fruits or vegetables that may be new to her. Healthy eating is very important in this family, and nothing that is not local and organically grown makes it to the fridge. As a result, Kira's palate is well developed for a toddler. This also makes family travels much easier, and Kira has already traveled to France, Morocco, the Caribbean, Mexico and within the States; feeding Kira abroad or away from home is not a hassle.

RIGHT: A mix and match of elements, from rustic and industrial bistro chairs to farm pendant lights, coexist happily for a modern yet inviting dining area.

OPPOSITE: A modern cupboard matching the kitchen colors adds more storage through the living room. A door to the garage doubles as a chalk memo board, making the space more personal.

Bread
- Potatoes
- Zuchini
- Cherry to
- Cel
- Maple Sir

KIRA

Apple Cider vinegar
Honey
gnochi

OPPOSITE: A modern gray wall contrasts with the all-white wall theme. A child-level coat rack below the upper rack allows Kira to hang her jackets and backpacks just like the grownups do.

ABOVE: By the entryway, a large calendar decorates the wall, while the Ikea storage trunk hides all of Kira's toys and toddler game collection.

Selwa and Ryan's bedroom has a calm, Scandinavian feel to it. Accents like the pompom bed throw and the Spanish bull figurine add some global flair.

Kira is an early bookworm. She listens to stories in both French and English whether she's with Mom or Dad.

THE
KIDS
ARE
ALL
RIGHT!

Kira's play-time corner, situated right by the kitchen, allows her to mimic her parents when it's dinner prep time. Hours of fun are spent in this little corner.

LEFT: Kira's doll Lola gets to try every cupcake recipe Kira cooks. Lola is also bilingual.

ABOVE: Kira's little tent is her quiet, cozy spot for listening to stories or impromptu napping.

In the backyard, Selwa and Kira spend a lot of time watching tomatoes grow. Kira loves to eat the ripe ones directly from the plant.

HAM AND CHEESE TART

MAKES 4 INDIVIDUAL TARTS

Homemade or store-bought puff pastry dough

Ham, thinly sliced

Salt

Pepper

Nutmeg, grated or ground

Grated cheese of your choice (we use a mix of mozzarella, pecorino, and provolone)

4 tablespoons heavy cream

Fresh thyme

Preheat your oven at 400° F.

On an oven grid (cooling rack), lay a piece of parchment paper. Set aside.

On a work surface, divide the dough into 4 squares; fold back the edges of each square, and with a fork, stab the center of the square and press on the borders to flatten out the edges.

To each tart, add some ham. Season with salt, pepper, and grated nutmeg to taste.

Sprinkle each tart with the grated cheese.

Gently pour 1 tablespoon heavy cream in the middle of each puff pastry square to moisten the center, but do not let the cream overflow on the sides.

Sprinkle the thyme on top of the tarts; then transfer tarts onto the parchment sheet.

Bake for 20 to 25 minutes. The tarts should look crisp and golden, and they may have risen during the cooking. Remove from the oven and let cool for 5 minutes before serving.

Note: This recipe can be adapted with various toppings. Selwa also recommends a parsley-garlic-mushroom with mozzarella combo. *Bon appétit!*

Claire + Stéphane

VIEUX-LILLE, FRANCE

FOUR YEARS AGO, Claire and Stéphane moved their family, including two sons, Léon and Louis, now ages twelve and fifteen, into a charming old house in the Vieux-Lille, the old part of this town of northern France. Their home has a lot of original features that Claire and Stéphane chose to leave intact, keeping the charm of the old.

After twenty years in the private sector and as an entrepreneur, Claire went through some difficult personal and professional events that forced her to reassess her priorities and radically change her perspective on work and life. She decided to take a break from a time-demanding and stressful career; Claire's difficult time in life marked the beginning of her personal "rebuilding." She started yoga and meditation, is pursuing a degree and is also starting a new business. She also enjoys spending more time at home with her loved ones, cherishing moments with her two teenage sons and being more available for them. "I get to see them when they're coming from school and can listen to stories of their day and their teenage lives, which I couldn't do when I was as a full-time working mom," adds Claire.

Claire and Stéphane's favorite room in their home is the kitchen. Here is where the family gathers, the boys do their homework and family memories are built. Breakfasts and dinners are always taken together. The family has a fun routine of sharing their "top-three-of-the-day," where each person shares the three most positive things that happened to them that day. "It's a great way," says Claire, "to listen to each other, to stay positive and to keep track of everyone's life and expe-riences." The kitchen is also open to the outdoors, and for Claire, having a direct view and access to the patio is priceless and refreshing.

Claire and Stéphane are big flea marketers and collectors: figurines, vintage plush toys, miniature cars and tennis rackets fill their living room shelves. They love to scout fleas on week-ends and while traveling abroad. "We are big kids deep down. We get excited about little objects, but the challenge is making a spot for our latest finds in our home," says Claire.

The couple's interior design goals are to create a home that "feels like them." They have no particular style in mind, but they like to curate objects from different eras and styles. They definitely use an intuitive approach to decorating their home: if it feels right, it's in! Stéphane is also very active in the decorating decision-making. As a creative—he works for a Web design agency—he has a natural eye for design and is active in the decision process. "We fill our home with objects that fit our style and taste, but it is also important for us to keep the soul of the home. The tiles in the entryway were cleaned and restored, as opposed to replaced, because we wanted to respect the charm of the old in this home," said Stéphane.

In their parenting philosophy, Claire and Stéphane want their sons to be curious learners. They often travel aboard to show their sons the world. The family is debating what the next destination will be: Léon, twelve, wants to visit Rio de Janeiro, while Louis, fifteen, is fascinated and intrigued by the city of Tokyo.

It's also crucial for Claire to teach her sons the value of things. She encourages them to save money to acquire their dream objects, and be patient: "Kids want everything very fast these days. I don't want my sons to fall into the pitfalls of overconsumption." Claire and Stéphane managed to create a space that reflects them, a refuge for their family that feels natural and authentic. It's not decorated to impress visitors or show off a collection; it comes truly from the heart. This home is definitely a happy nest for a happy bunch.

OPPOSITE: The kitchen, with its original French tiled floors, white and blue wall tiles and door molding details, plays with modern elements, like the wooden dinnerware cabinet and modern floor lamp.
ABOVE LEFT: Claire used a lost spot on top of the stairs to add a mini desk corner. To visually delineate the space, she cleverly chose a graphic mustard wallpaper and painted a French bistro chair in a bright shade of red.

Claire + Stéphane 257

The kitchen, open to the outdoors, is Claire and Stéphane's favorite room in the house and where most of the family's moments happen. The gorgeous floor tiles are original to the house. Claire thrifted a vintage French armchair and deliberately kept its old upholstery to preserve the character of the piece: if this armchair could speak, it would have so many stories to tell!

It was important for Claire and Stéphane to let the house speak, embracing its past and soul. The wooden moldings retained in the dining area give the space a grand French chateau vibe.

The entryway was also brought back to its original glory. Instead of retiling, the couple cleaned the entire floor and tiles to give them a new life. A deep cleaning and sanding brought back a glorious patina to the stairs.

Claire and Stéphane's simply furnished bedroom showcases more vintage and original building features: the brick wall and built-in wooden dresser were cleaned and left deliberately raw to let the house tells its story.

OPPOSITE: Louis chose a red retro wallpaper for his room. The old chimney, now unusable, was creatively repurposed as a bookcase.

BELOW: Claire explained that when Louis requested a new computer, they asked him to save his money and do his research. He built spreadsheets comparing key features and showing prices differences among different computer models; it became a dedicated project. He was so excited when he had gathered enough money. In fact, Louis decided to build his computer, and it became a bonding project with his father. Son and dad spent an extensive time building the computer of Louis's dream. It meant a whole lot more to Louis than if we had gone to the store to buy a computer.

Léon is an avid Smurfs collector and a bookworm, so his room is a great reflection of his hobbies. The soft palette of the diamond-checkered wallpaper and soft palette complement more of the family's vintage finds from flea markets.

TARTE TATIN

The tarte Tatin is an upside-down pastry in which the fruit (apples in this case) is caramelized in butter and sugar before the tart is baked. Legend has it that the Tatin sisters in France accidentally baked an apple pie upside down, only to discover the happy accident they had just invented.

SERVES 4 TO 6

²/₃ cup (150g) butter

1 cup (200g) sugar

6–8 apples

1 frozen puff pastry dough,
    thawed

Using a Tatin dish or cast iron skillet on the stovetop, put your butter in to melt over low heat and add the sugar.

Peel the apples and cut them in thin slices. Arrange apple slices in the dish on top of the melted butter/sugar mixture. Start at the center of the dish and work concentrically until the bottom of the dish is completely covered.

Preheat the oven to 350° F.

Bake the tarte until the caramel appears, approximately 15 to 20 minutes. The color should be a golden brown. Make sure it doesn't burn.

Remove tarte from the oven and let it cool down a bit. Then place the puff pastry dough on top of the dish, covering the caramel apple slices. Tuck in the dough on the sides. Bake tarte in the oven for 20 to 25 minutes.

If the puff dough rose during cooking, don't pierce it, it will come down by itself.

When cooked, turn the tart upside down onto a serving dish. Serve with crème fraîche or vanilla ice cream.

First Edition
25 24 23 22   5 4 3 2

Published by
Gibbs Smith
P.O. Box 667
Layton, Utah 84041
1.800.835.4993 orders
www.gibbs-smith.com

Designed by Sheryl Dickert
Printed and bound in China

Gibbs Smith books are printed on either recycled, 100% post-
consumer waste, FSC-certified papers or on paper produced
from sustainable PEFC-certified forest/controlled wood source.
Learn more at www.pefc.org.

Library of Congress Control Number: 2017951233
ISBN 978-1-4236-4816-1

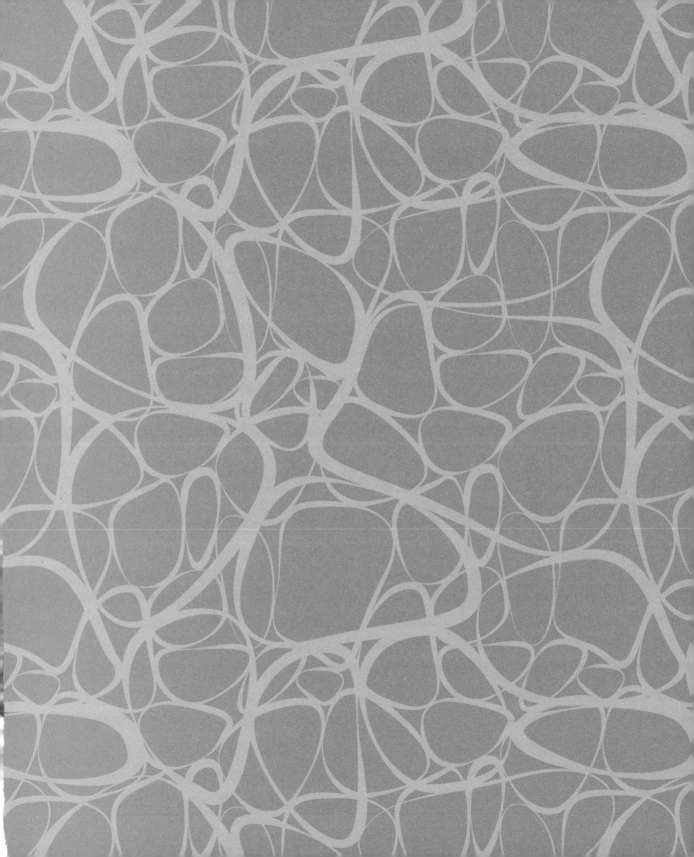

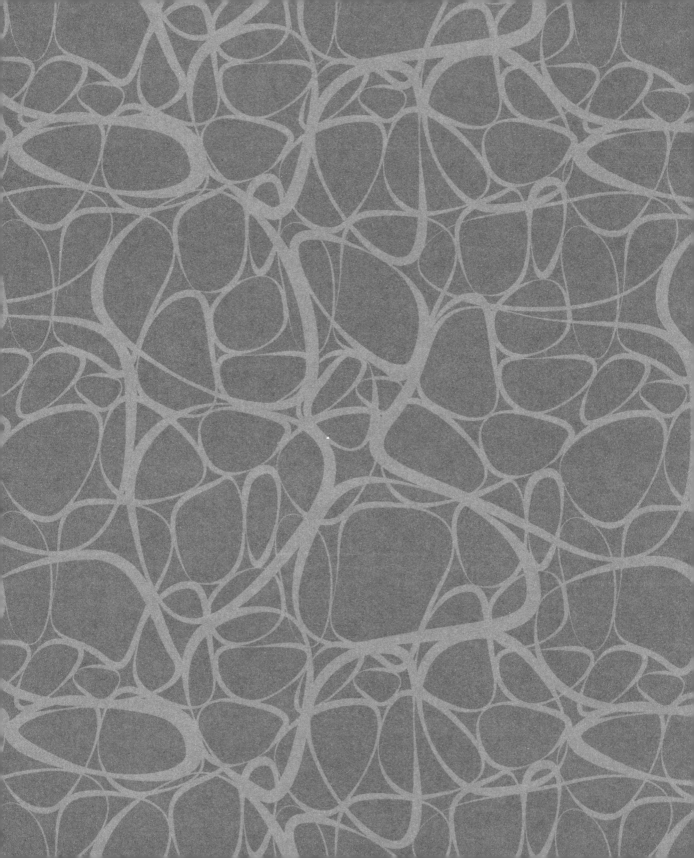